CW00972108

THE TRIAL OF LOKI:

a study in
Nordic heathen morality

by

Alan James

First published 1997

Second Australian edition 2013

© 2013 by Renewal Publications
ISBN   978-1-300-60009-1

This revised edition corrects obvious typographical errors in the original, but retains the author's spelling of proper nouns. Commentary on the original text is provided in footnotes by the editor.

Contents

Introduction

1997 edition   *first U.S. edition*   *2012 U.S. edition*

The material in this work was first published in serial form in the Australian Odinist journal, *Renewal*. Its first outing as a booklet occurred in 1997. Retail sales were restricted to Australia, but complimentary copies were sent to, among others, all academics working on Old Norse studies in English-speaking universities. Comments from the general public were entirely favourable. By contrast, not a single taxpayer-funded academic so much as acknowledged receipt.

A few reviews appeared in avowedly heathen publications. I thought the most interesting one was this, by Gárman Lord, in Volume 14 Number 3 of *Théod Magazine*:

> One of the most vexing dilemmas faced by Ásatrú today is that, on the one hand, it is a religion that depends heavily upon its historical lore rather than its historical continuity for its credentials of religious validity, and on the other hand,

this lore upon which it depends is not very accessible. It is an extremely fragmentary lore, written down in extinct languages under circumstances grossly deformed by considerations of taboo, both Heathen and Christian. It is also, for the most part, an inherently difficult lore, full of ideas that would still be quite esoterically challenging even if written down in Modern English in a way that was both straightforward and complete. And when the average American Ásatrúer peruses it on his own, what does he get from it? Plenty of pleasure, to be sure, but also some very strange ideas; a groundling's eye view of what surely must once have been a noble, exalted, subtle and sophisticated religion, in which groundling view, all too often, the lofty wisdom of Óðinn is apt to be reduced to mere treacherous duplicity and low cunning, Thórr becomes a rude, oafishly stupid buffoon, Freya little more than a layabout celestial slut, and a god like Loki, with his seemingly inexhaustible bag of tricks, perhaps the wisest, cleverest, most real, approachable and intelligible deity of all! Whatever power the old tales may or may not still have, they certainly do seem to retain the power of being a kind of mirror!

Is this, however, at the very least, faithful to our elderfathers' view of these same gods and this same religion, based upon this same elder corpus? Not likely. No religion as morally and ethically confused as the modern American Ásatrú revival could serve a real historical folk very well or be likely to be around very long, and there surely must have been a great deal more to it all than the kind of moral confusion and perversity not just reflected in modem Ásatrú email traffic, but often in the journals themselves. In fact, it sometimes seems that a "Loki cult" of the kind that is nowhere documented amongst our elderen is the most viable and growing feature of today's Ásatrú. This is an aspect on which Alan James' book seems to offer no direct comment ... at least, not within the lines of his prose itself. His analysis of *Lokasenna* is far more cautious and circumspect than that. Whether it is also a "penetrating" analysis is a question that must be left to those much more up on the scholarly-analytical literature than I am. Even so, however, this Australian writer pulls few punches about the judgments that he does seem willing to offer.

Trial takes a really focused look at the dynamics at work amongst the gods in *Lokasenna,* at the poem's relentlessly "legalistic" tone, at its queer failure on the part of the gods to defend themselves adequately against Loki's increasingly twisted and debased accusations, and at the place of *Loksenna* in the flow of other related lore, from all of which James seems to infer that it looks to him like a case of Loki being "set up" by gods who are in fact cleverer than Loki, who know what is about to happen to him by the weaving of Wyrd, whether Loki himself does or not, and who are only too eager to make themselves the agents of such vengeful justice. And though James himself does not say as much, we could say after a reading that if this really were a trial today, Loki might well be found not guilty by reason of insanity. It is ironic that many American Ásatrúers today seem to be heard deriving many a theological truth of their religion out of the lies of Loki in poetry like *Lokasenna,* in ways that may well run dead opposite to the far more sophisticated points that the unknown ancient skald was really trying to make. Just like poor Loki himself, they are being had on too!

It would seem that the fate of great art, which is what James seems to consider *Lokasenna* and its ilk to be, is sometimes just not to be understood, at least by the modern Ásatrú groundling community. By James' interpretation, taken together with *Balder's Dream* and the rest of the cycle, what *Lokasenna* is really trying to tell us is the psychological tale of the progressive deterioration of a sociopathic, perhaps psychopathic personality, from mere heavenly mischief-maker to deicide bound down on a rock for the crime of conspiring to destroy the cosmos for the gratification of his own sick monster ego, as a compelling kind of allegory of showing us why human society, in the end, can never really "work", in such a fashion as if to say we shouldn't feel too bad; society never really "worked" amongst the gods either, and for exactly the same reasons! Certainly a very dark view, though really not presented as such by James, but, if true, also a masterful medieval literary tour-de-force! In any case, a view that offers much food for thought; by all means, get and read the booklet if you possibly can!

Just for the record, I *did* consider the idea of Loki pleading insanity (as Gárman Lord suggested above) when I argued that Frigg offered Loki the chance to plead "diminished responsibility". Loki chose not to do so. Again, purely for the record, I do not agree with the "dark" allegory of human society suggested at the end of Gárman's review. As far as I can understand it, the overall trend in all the Germanic eschatology is for improvement.

Of all the letters I have received from readers, there have been many that queried this or that aspect of my reading of *Lokasenna*. The only one that was overtly hostile came from the self-described Swiss shaman and Loki-devotee, Fuensanta Plaza. Fuensanta died in early 2010, so I can't seek her permission to reprint her intriguing letter here, but my reply was as follows:

3 January 2005

Dear Fuensanta Plaza,

Thank you for taking the trouble to send me your interesting critique of *The Trial of Loki*.

Yes, I am aware of what Stephen Pollington, and many others, wrote about flyting in general. I happen to dispute that these general statements apply to *Lokasenna*. My basic reason is that mere flyting can hardly explain the extraordinarily rich structure of the poem. The ordering of the participants, and their differing responses to Loki's attacks, suggest that it is a carefully crafted (almost choreographed) composition, a work of art with a higher purpose than mere pointless entertainment. If that is so, then we need to ask what that purpose was. I do not claim that my interpretation is necessarily correct. Or, as I said in the essay: "If it is

iv

possible to provide a consistent reading of *Lokasenna*, not necessarily *the* correct reading but at least one in which heathen expectations about the behaviour of the gods are addressed, then the place of the poem in the corpus of late Norse paganism will be shown to require reappraisal." Someone else's alternative reading may be better, although I have yet to encounter one that is. At any rate, the point is that the poem seems to *mean something*.

I didn't think I *was* "making one [god] all good and the other all evil". I was simply trying to suggest a rational reading of the drama presented to us within this one poem. A rational reading implies that the "characters" in it speak when they do, and say what they say, for reasons that can be related to their own natures and functions and destinies – and ultimately to Fate. It's no more to do with good or evil than is the ambition of the king in *Macbeth*. We accept that Macbeth behaves in certain ways precisely because we know that he is Macbeth and not, say, Ophelia. If *Lokasenna* is genuinely a work of art, as I believe, then it is reasonable to ask why goddess *X* says *Y* at line *Z*. This involves trying to see the situation from her point of view. And that is what I tried to do. I think this is far more fruitful than taking the poem as either an indictment of the gods (McKinnell) or just another bit of coarse flyting (most writers before McKinnell). Of course, my interpretation is confined to *Lokasenna* itself, on the terms that *Lokasenna* presents to us. A balanced view of the overall role of Loki in the eschatological picture would require surveying *all* the literary and other evidence.

Incidentally, I also disagree with Pollington's statement (which you approvingly underlined when quoting it), that in flyting "… the preliminary incident is in fact beyond dispute". There are plenty of examples to the contrary. One will have to suffice here. In *Njál's saga* Skarpheðin threw some women's underwear at Flosi, saying Flosi needed them because "… people say that you are the bride of the Svínfell's troll every ninth night, and thus he makes a woman of you." Norwegian law of precisely this period penalised with outlawry any man "…who says something about another man which cannot be, nor come to be, nor have been: declares he is a woman every ninth night or has had a child..." Even the *law* recognised that Skarpheðin's verbal attack on Flosi was not just *not* "beyond dispute". It was in fact impossible!

Before closing, I can't recall having seen Gary Stanfield's review of my essay, so thanks for quoting from it. I don't know whether you saw the Australian or the American edition of the booklet, but the Australian edition carried a warning on the back cover: "... this new reading of a heathen poem might shock and dismay traditionalists".

Finally, despite your accusation, I don't "dislike" Loki. I merely tried to make greater sense of one poem than other people have in the past. That poem is in turn only one piece of evidence as to how our ancestors may have viewed both Fate and the gods – including Loki.

Wassail! - Alan James

In 2011, Ingwine of White Marsh Press in the United States kindly published a second American edition of *The Trial of Loki*. As far as I have seen, this has not led to any reviews as insightful as that by Gárman Lord. But neither has it elicited any hostile mail.

This new, second Australian edition expands very slightly on some points that helpful readers have told me were originally made too tersely. Some readers have also called for a translation of the original poem to be included. I think the appended version here, by that great American lawyer Henry Adams Bellows, gives a strong feeling for the original rollicking tone. As always, that can only be achieved at the sacrifice of some word-for-word accuracy: hence the difference between Bellows' version and some of the quotes in my essay.

Alan James
Melbourne, 2013

Lokasenna - background and problems

The poem *Lokasenna* is preserved in the Codex Regius, a vellum manuscript written in Iceland in the second half of the thirteenth century.

Lokasenna is usually thought to have been composed in the tenth century, although it possibly contains some traces of more recent additions during a late stage of its oral transmission. While its precise date and origin are unknown, its author clearly had a good working knowledge of Germanic mythology, of a nature suggesting that he lived in the late heathen period. After a thorough study of the internal evidence, Einarr Sveinsson concluded that the poem was composed no later than 1000 AD.

For every fragment of heathen literature that has survived we have to be grateful to the Christian scribes who went to the trouble (and possibly risk) of writing it down. Given the fact of this Christian filter it is not surprising that no significant poetry of heathen devotion has been recorded. Anyone who searches among what the scribes saw fit to preserve for poems about the beauty, glory or anguish of the gods will be disappointed. We know that Freyja's search for her departed husband was marked by tears of gold, so rich and fertile was she perceived to be. Yet the surviving literature is silent on her sufferings. All that is left to us is a metaphor for gold:

"Freyja's tears". The full story, beautiful as it must have been, was evidently deemed too powerful to be allowed to survive.

The heathen literature that the scribes chose to preserve is often grotesque, and usually portrays the Nordic deities reaching the limits of their powers. That is neither surprising nor necessarily malicious. After all, the Christian scribes had an entirely different philosophy of life to the heathen bards.

One very important difference between these outlooks was that although the heathens believed the world of gods and men to be ruled by Fate, they added that those with the courage and free will to assert themselves might in some ways rise above the very Fate that destroys them. This was the heathen understanding of heroism. We see it in *Hávamál* ("Wealth perishes, kinfolk perish, one's very self perishes, but fame never dies for him who gets it worthily"), in the Anglo-Saxon gnomic verse (*Dom bið selast* – "Fame is the best of all"), and in *Beowulf* (lines 1386 onward).

Christianity consciously overturned this philosophy. The Christian universe was governed by a skewed concept of Justice, not Fate. The idea that a hero, or a deity, might sacrifice everything in a foredoomed fight against implacable odds held little appeal to the new philosophy. After all, the cosmic order was now seen as just. Any being opposing it was therefore yielding to one or another "sin".

Given this contrast between the two philosophies it is no surprise that the Christian scribes would have found it appropriate to preserve those heathen poems that portrayed the old deities asserting themselves against Fate. Any such poem would have been seen through the new ideological lens as evidence that the deities were themselves flawed – "sinful" rather than "heroic".

Perhaps the strangest of all the surviving heathen poems is *Lokasenna*. From the new Christian viewpoint *Lokasenna* probably seemed to be an instance of the Old Norse bards condemning their own pagan gods through Loki's indictment. No doubt they thought it made for good propaganda against the old religion.

The poem is set during a banquet in Ægir's hall. Loki has not been invited, but he gatecrashes the affair anyway, and proceeds to insult every god and goddess present. One after the other the accused deities protest against Loki's slanders, but the confrontation is only resolved when the previously absent Þórr returns and forces Loki to flee. Loki is then captured and bound, according to the concluding prose passage.

Many modern scholars have commented on this poem. It must always be born in mind that modern academics specialising in Old Norse literature were usually raised in a broadly Christian context and consequently most of them are hostile to the heathen material. Usually they see it as demonstrating the breakdown of the social and moral boundaries of existence under the older moral dispensation. Perhaps the most systematic exposition of this argument in recent decades has been that of John McKinnell (1987-8 and 1994). McKinnell sees Loki as an institutionalised "Accuser" who exposes the gods as having "self-serving motives" for which they are "rightly humiliated".

McKinnell's reading of the poem is consistent, perceptive and at times ingenious. It also raises an obvious problem. If *Lokasenna* can really be dated to the late heathen period, we have to assume that the poem had some sort of moral relevance for its audience – a relevance that may not have been as obvious to the Christian scribe who wrote it down (either accurately or in an amended form) three hundred years later in the *Codex Regius*.

McKinnell's approach to the poem suggests that a heathen

audience could really have believed that the apparently "flawed" deities of *Lokasenna* were somehow justified in their treatment of Loki. If so, we must ask how. From a modern point of view *Lokasenna* seems to travesty the very notion of heathen divinity. On the other hand, its metre seems very early for an Old Norse poem, and it has the feel of being an anciently rooted heathen drama. It almost cries out to be acted on a simple stage, such as dais before the "cuneus" at the Odinist cult centre of Yeavering, Northumbria.

The purpose of this essay is, therefore, to investigate whether *Lokasenna* could have made any moral sense to a late tenth-century heathen audience.

Characterisation and perspective

In modern literature we seldom accept a character's self-assessment at face value. The key characters, the ones whose moves determine the plot of the story as it unfolds, and who therefore set the overall mood, may reveal their character strengths and failings through their words or deeds. Fictional characters, even the ostensible heroes, can and frequently do condemn themselves out of their own mouths. A well-known example of this occurs in Tom Wolfe's 1988 novel *The Bonfire of the Vanities*, in which the twists of the plot progressively reveal that those traits of which the main character is initially proud amount to little more than greed and amoral vanity.

In religious or mythological literature, however, the modern western reader, conditioned largely by the Bible, is perhaps less likely to be sceptical about such self-assessment, especially when the author appears to acquiesce in the character's view of himself. Following the Biblical account of David, for instance, we tend to accept that king's sordid secular deeds as being in some way motivated by worthy religious intentions – simply because he is presented in the Bible as a "hero".

Loki is the main character in *Lokasenna*. His is the voice in 32 of the 65 stanzas. It is Loki's decision to return to Ægir's hall, Loki who wishes to stir up strife and hate, and Loki who chooses the moral ground on which to assail the individual gods and goddesses in turn. At this structural level, the poem tempts us to identify with Loki – or at least to give him the same sort of sympathetic hearing that we initially extend to Tom Wolfe's modern fictional creation.

McKinnell's analysis seems to take Loki at face value. According to McKinnell's reading, Loki's purpose is simple. He wishes to provoke a final confrontation with the gods in order to hasten Ragnarök. The gods, for their part, wish to placate Loki in order to defer Ragnarök – for some unexplained reason. One after another the gods and goddesses give placatory or seemingly ineffective responses to Loki's taunts, and only succeed in confirming that there is some form of truth in Loki's accusations. At last Þórr returns from the East. His repeated threats force Loki to flee, after which he is pursued, caught and bound.

McKinnell's blow by blow interpretation of the structure of this poem, including the tactics of why certain gods choose to enter the altercation at specific points, makes a great deal of sense. If we also assume that Loki does not understand Fate, that he cannot foresee the outcome of Ragnarök, McKinnell's understanding of Loki's motives is at least totally consistent. It does not, however, shed much light on the motives of the gods and goddesses.

On this reading of the poem the deities are, at best, gullible victims of Loki's provocation, and Þórr, by causing the final rupture, "is merely stupid". Noting that the poem "gives no hint of" the renewed and purified world after Ragnarök that we glimpse in *Völuspá*, a poem that was clearly familiar to the author of *Lokasenna*, McKinnell argues that "... the gods have it in their power to delay Ragnarök indefinitely; after they have driven Loki out and subsequently bound him, the initiative passes out of their hands".

And yet it is clear that Fate is a major theme in *Lokasenna*. It is announced from the moment at which Óðinn tells Víðarr to make space for the Wolf's father, and is alluded to many times after that. Most of the gods clearly understand Fate, and there is no obvious reason why they should want to delay it. There is also no particular reason to insist that they have it in their power to delay Ragnarök. After all, with Baldr dead before the poem begins, everything leading up to Ragnarök has already been set in motion.

Perhaps the argument that McKinnell puts forward could be seen as being merely Loki's misunderstanding of the situation. But the actual poem, *Lokasenna,* does not insist that we accept Loki's view of either himself or the gods. Given that a contemporary audience would have been aware of the punishment that Loki is to bring upon himself by his scandalous outbursts, it may be possible that the author of this remarkable poem had a more complex purpose in mind than even McKinnell's subtle analysis concedes. At the very least we should remain aware that, however the Loki character in the poem sees things, we are not obliged to accept his perspective. Perhaps the Æsir are wiser than Loki thinks, and perhaps the poet would have expected a contemporary audience to assume as much.

If it is valid to suggest that the poet may have intended to subvert Loki, perhaps to show him up as a traitor who fully deserves the treatment that the gods mete out, then we should ask whether there can be another explanation of why the deities tolerate his provocations for so long, an explanation in which the gods' behaviour is honourable on heathen terms. As McKinnell says: "Verbal contests in Eddic poetry are not motiveless, but have some practical intention and result". It could be added that in all other such contests, the gods win.

Is *Lokasenna* really an exception?

Nið in Lokasenna

To place the poem in its literary context, *Lokasenna* takes the form of a *senna*, which Preben Meulengracht Sørensen (1983) defines as a quarrel in which "two or more people accuse each other of despicable qualities or actions". This attempt to cast scorn on the other side doesn't necessarily involve *nið*, but it frequently does. *Nið* in turn "signifies gross insults of a symbolic kind", usually through suggestions that the male who is attacked has the contemptible moral characteristics that Germanic society associated with passive homosexuality. In the case of a female victim she could be accused of being perverted or lecherous, or else of having sex with the accuser, which is psychologically equated with the violation of her husband's sexual integrity.

Many of Loki's scurrilous insults in *Lokasenna* are of this order. The modem reader may be tempted to regard them as coarse sub-Rabelaisian burlesque. To dismiss them so lightly, though, is rather like travelling in a foreign country without ever having quite realised that one is abroad. If, instead, we choose to enter the moral and legal world of *Lokasenna*, we find that Loki's insults take on a much more serious hue. They are *nið* pure and simple, and *nið* was not something to be taken lightly. In 12th and 13th century Iceland *nið* was a killing matter.

Meulengracht Sørensen points out that: "The right of

vengeance prescribed for [*nið*-type] slanders is the least conditional in Icelandic law. It holds good in only two other situations, namely in a case of killing and ... in a case of sexual relations, forced or otherwise, with a close woman relative of the man to whom the right of vengeance is allowed. The most serious verbal offences are thus equated with killing, rape and adultery, and are regarded as more flagrant than, for instance, bodily injury".

Numerous examples in Icelandic literature suggest that a man who does not attempt to refute the accusation of *nið* through physical combat is regarded as *a niðingr*. If he is not prepared to defend himself physically against these shameful accusations, it is as if he may as well be regarded as having committed them, or at least as being not averse to committing them.

Furthermore, *bauchling*, a set of customs very like those associated with *nið*, prevailed on the borders of England and Scotland until heathenism was finally curtailed there following the union of the crowns. As in Iceland, the accused was regarded as being contemptible. In 1563 a law was passed against *bauchling*, so it must have still been common at that time. The condemnation of shameful acts was one of the last aspects of heathen morality to require legal proscription by the Christians, from which we can deduce that the avoidance of this type of shame was very important to the heathens.

Yet in *Lokasenna* nearly all the gods are accused of shameful acts, and none of them kills Loki, as they would otherwise have been perfectly entitled to do. Why not?

One obvious explanation is that they know they can't. Having a fore-knowledge of Fate, they are aware that Loki will not be killed until Ragnarök. But they also know, and Skaði makes it plain, that Loki is destined to be bound until the final battle. Why then don't they seize him as soon as he forces his way back into Ægir's Hall? Unless the poem is to be regarded as nothing more than a verbal way of killing time, ultimately a meaningless diversion, they must have a reason.

The analysis that comprises section four of this paper is not intended to provide a definitive answer to these questions, but rather to set up a new avenue of interrogation. If it is possible to provide a consistent reading of *Lokasenna,* not necessarily the correct reading but at least one in which heathen expectations about the behaviour of the gods are addressed, then the place of this poem in the corpus of late Norse paganism will be shown to require reappraisal.

In brief, I will suggest that Loki re-enters Ægir's hall for reasons to which we have no direct access, and are ultimately irrelevant, but which may be very similar to those outlined by McKinnell. Regardless of Loki's reasons, the gods and goddesses have a purpose of their own, which is essentially to try Loki for treason. They allow him to establish his hostility, and while giving him the fairest possible hearing they manoeuvre him into boasting of his guilt. Yet they are unable to seize him because they have sworn that Ægir's hall is a place of sanctuary. Only Þórr is permitted to break this oath, and he is away in the East. The gods therefore attempt to keep Loki talking until Þórr returns. For his part, Loki maintains a tirade of *nið*-type slanders against the gods in the hope of at least gaining some sort of psychological victory by provoking them into breaking their oaths. The temptation is strong, especially for Freyr, but his anger is diffused by Byggvir; and Loki is kept howling indignities at the gods until Þórr returns, engages Loki in a test of courage, and compels him to flee from the hall. Once outside Loki can be, and is, legitimately bound. Justice has not only been done, but has been seen to be done.

The Senna of *Lokasenna*

The opening of *Lokasenna* suggests the pre-trial legal skirmishes that are sometimes heard in modern courtrooms. Since we learn later that the poem is set after the death of Baldr and before the punishment of Loki, this legalistic (I will argue courtroom) feeling is not inappropriate, and has been noted by several writers, including Klingenberg 1983 and Meulengracht Sørensen 1988.

Bragi opens by declaring that the Æsir will never offer Loki a seat at the feast. Óðinn, reminded by Loki that the two were once foster brothers, over-rules Bragi. At the very beginning of the action, then, Óðinn affirms impartial rules – in this case those of foster-brotherhood and hospitality. Bragi has effectively argued that Loki doesn't deserve a hearing because his enormity is known to all, but Óðinn immediately positions himself above this viewpoint. At the same time, of course, Óðinn grimly reminds Loki of how their destinies will eventually converge in the form of the Wolf. It is hard to see why Óðinn would say this unless he is giving a form of judicial warning. If so, his statement could mean something like this: "I know all the rules and precedents, and I also understand Fate. Bear this in mind if you rely on our foster-brotherhood to allow you to cause trouble at this gathering."

Bragi then makes an attempt at conciliation. He offers Loki a horse and a sword if he will be silent. McKinnell draws attention to the fact that Bragi's offer is couched in legal language. Whatever the offer may have meant in terms of heathen law, Loki rejects it anyway, claiming that Bragi is too poor to meet his side of the deal. The audience of the poem, however, knows that Bragi is of "splendid appearance", a phrase that seems to suggest material wealth. Furthermore, if Bragi's offer is made in an official rather than personal capacity, it is immaterial whether Bragi himself can afford the payment. Either way, by refusing even to consider Bragi's offer, Loki already begins to look like he may be setting himself up for a fall.

Having complied with the formal requirements, Bragi is then free to observe that if the hospitality rules didn't apply, he would be happy to deal with Loki personally. There is no reason to believe that Bragi doesn't mean exactly what he says. As Bellows commented: "… poetry, of which Bragi was the patron, was generally associated in the Norse mind with peculiar valor, and most of the skaldic poets were likewise noted fighters". Loki remarks that Bragi can fight him if he wants to. Of course, that option is not open. Óðinn has already ruled that the laws of hospitality *do* apply, and Bragi has just yielded to Óðinn's ruling. Loki's invitation to Bragi is therefore just petty bluster.

Iðunn then accuses both Loki and Bragi of being tactless. In the course of this rebuke, she reminds Bragi that Loki is an adoptive relative of the Æsir who has to be tolerated for the sake of everyone else whose relationship to the Æsir is of this type. This brings us back to the theme of foster-brotherhood that has dominated proceedings so far, but perhaps raises it to a new level. Loki may claim the rights of the *brøðurbani,* but unlike the Æsir's other adoptive kinsmen he is showing little inclination to respect the obligations implied. If Iðunn also understands Fate, she knows that Loki will soon place himself formally beyond any protection that foster-brotherhood may provide. One way or another, Iðunn is foreshadowing a distinction between those who are worthy of being adoptive kinsmen and those who forsake their rights through their own actions.

Loki replies that Iðunn made love to her brother's slayer. This is a strange accusation, although it does set the low tone of most of Loki's subsequent allegations. McKinnell interprets it to mean that "Being friendly to adoptive kinsmen is all very well, but making one's brother's killer into one of them by having sex with him is carrying it a bit too far". If that is indeed Loki's meaning, then he has fallen into Iðunn's trap by agreeing with her. If he claims to draw the line at a mere sexual act, no matter how treacherous he is able to represent it, then the deeds that he is later to boast of are well beyond this limit. (Of course, there may well be references here, as elsewhere, to other and perhaps morally complex legends that have not survived.)

Having made her point, Iðunn then withdraws from the argument with a reminder to Bragi not to fight Loki. If Bragi really is a hot-tempered god, rather than the coward that Loki has accused him of being, this makes sense. No action taken against Loki can be valid until Loki has crossed the line and destroyed his own protected status.

Gefjun takes up this theme by calling Loki and Bragi "you two Æsir". As with the modern legal presumption of innocence, Loki remains one of the Æsir, and has to be treated as such, until he is clearly shown to have overstepped the mark. If Gefjun's next comment means that Bragi's threats were not meant seriously, she may be trying to give Loki the confidence to proceed with his case. After all, we learn later that Loki will not fight when a genuine opportunity is presented to him. If her comment actually means that Bragi is quarrelsome but the gods are aware of that and make allowance, she is again encouraging Loki to continue.

In response, Loki accuses Gefjun of having prostituted herself for a jewel. Whether there is any form of truth in this charge – perhaps at a symbolic level – is irrelevant: Loki has now made it clear that on his own terms the exchange of sexual services for a consideration is a grave charge. Loki then foolishly invites Óðinn to speak by parodying an expression used in *Hávamál*. Whereas Gunnloð had "laid her arm over" Óðinn, Loki tells Gefjun that she "laid [her] thigh over" the supplier of the jewel.

Óðinn might be expected to respond in anger. Instead, he reminds Loki that Gefjun knows Fate. If the poem regards Óðinn as a wise god, this can have only one meaning. Loki is being formally reminded of the gravity of the situation in which he has placed himself. It is as if a modern judge half-way through a trial were to break off proceedings to remind a witness of the laws relating to perjury.

At this point Loki would be well-advised to heed the judicial warning. Instead he attacks the validity of Fate itself. As the chooser of those who will be slain in battle to join the ranks of the *einherjar*, Óðinn is one of Fate's agents. But Óðinn chooses only the best warriors, and Loki says this is unjust. Both the assembled Æsir and the audience of the poem know that the *einherjar* are doomed to fall in **this** life precisely because they **are** the best, and they are required for a higher purpose: the gods need their help to ensure that the forces of chaos are ultimately defeated. In short, despite Loki's absurd claim, Óðinn is adept at choosing the best warriors. By rejecting the higher, cosmic justice of this aspect of Fate, and satirising it in mundane human terms, Loki is treading on very thin ice. To reject Fate in this way is also to challenge the validity of the gods – and that validity now constitutes Loki's only protection.

If a modern person accused of contempt of court were to respond by strenuously denying the authority of the court that was trying him, he would be a fool. Loki is now such a fool. That he is worse we soon see. Having already proclaimed that the alleged sexual indiscretions of Iðunn and Gefjun are damning, Loki has prepared for himself a trap that any hearer of the poem could have foreseen. Óðinn now springs that trap. Compared to anything of which the two goddesses could be accused, Loki is an absolute pervert. Not only has he changed sex, but he even served as a subterranean milkmaid for eight years. (According to Meulengracht Sorensen this "must certainly be taken to mean that Loki served as a mistress to giants or trolls, whose sexuality was considered gross and unbridled".)

Loki counters that, in effect, his sexual perversion is no worse than Óðinn's working of a form of magic that would bring **human** male practitioners into disrepute. Once again he is sawing at his own lifeline by dissociating himself from the higher purposes that the Æsir represent, and which Óðinn's magical quests are undertaken in order to serve. In equating his own low lusts with Óðinn's necessary self-sacrifices, Loki has only underlined the vast moral difference between the two foster-brothers. He might as well have alleged that hanging on the wind-swept tree was an act of masochistic auto-eroticism.

Frigg now throws Loki a possible line of defence. She points out that the deeds of both Óðinn and Loki were fated anyway. Loki can safely back out at this point by saying he can't help being what he is. In refusing this offer to plead diminished responsibility Loki implicitly stands by his own past. He then accuses Frigg of having sex with Óðinn's brothers. Once more, Loki reveals his self-alienation by equating the actions of the gods with paltry human sexual sins. If there is any substance to his accusation at all, it would presumably have been based on some myth in which Frigg's actions were cosmically positive. If there is no such mythical basis, Loki is simply becoming boring. He seems unable to think of any insults that don't involve accusations of sleeping around.

Frigg replies that if she had a son "like Baldr" here, Loki would regret that accusation. We know, as all the gods who understand Fate know, as Loki knows, as the poem knows, and as its audience would have known, that Baldr isn't available to avenge her insult. All parties also know why. Likewise, we know that Frigg has another son, or perhaps stepson, "like Baldr", who isn't here just at the moment, but who might well be here soon. The response that Loki makes to this statement will determine the future shape of the poem – and of the larger eschatology. Loki, however, has lost all self-control. Yes, he crows, like a petty crook in the dock, Baldr isn't here – and he's not here because of me!

This should be the logical turning point of the poem. If these suggestions regarding the gods' motives have been more or less correct so far, Loki is "banged to rights". He has been afforded every legal protection, has confessed to his deeds, has refused to put in a lesser guilty plea, and has made it clear that he shows defiance rather than remorse.

All that remains now is for the gods to pass sentence. Why then do they not punish Loki at this point? They certainly have no further responsibilities to him, but Loki's virtual self-conviction may not override other moral obligations that they are obliged to follow. Ægir's hall is still a place of sanctuary. Only one of the Æsir seems to have the specific moral right to disregard oaths and vows when the situation requires it. *Voluspá* 26 suggests that this is one of Þórr's special roles, and Loki himself recognises this later, in stanza 64. But Þórr is not yet present.

What would a modern judge do if, for some reason, there were no police or prison authorities in the court to take charge of the prisoner whose own words had just convicted him? Maybe try to keep the prisoner talking, in the hope that the missing officials would turn up sooner or later. This is exactly what the gods do. It is perhaps significant that from this point in the poem there are no more legal quibbles. It seems to be relevant, also, that there is a literary precedent for this stalling technique: Þórr himself uses it in *Alvíssmál*, keeping the dwarf talking until the sun destroys him. This parallel, between Þórr keeping the dwarf waiting for the sun and the gods keeping the traitor waiting for Þórr, seems irresistible.

Given that Loki has been almost obsessive in making sexual allegations against other goddesses, Freyja is shrewd to speak up at this point. If anything can hold Loki's attention now, it is the easy target that Freyja presents to his degraded mind. It scarcely matters what she says, as long as she can engage him. In fact, though, what she chooses to say is relevant. Loki must be mad because Frigg, she reminds him, understands Fate. This statement, made at this point in the poem, seems to mean that Loki has fallen into Frigg's trap.

Loki's response is tediously predictable. He accuses Freyja of having slept with every male present. As a goddess concerned with sexuality Freyja would have failed her own divine duties if she had not in some sense shared a holy aspect of her sexuality with others. In reducing this sacred obligation to the level of a fishwife shrieking at her neighbour over the back fence, Loki succeeds only in displaying his own coarseness and vulgarity. That may not worry Loki, but to the poem's audience it confirms that Loki is not fit to share the company of the gods.

Njörðr cleverly sticks to Loki's favourite subject. What his daughter may do is *válítit*, harmless, but Loki's perversions are shameful. This technique works. Loki feels obliged to counter-attack. Njörðr, he says, came to Ásgarðr as a hostage. What's more, Hymir's daughters urinated in his mouth. As Óðinn, at least, knows, Njörðr will return to Vanaheim after Ragnarök, while Loki will be destroyed (Vafðrúnismál 39, 4-6). As to the claim about Hymir's daughters, one starts to wonder whether Loki really is by now crazy, as Freyja has just suggested. No myth survives that could be twisted, even by Loki, into this accusation. It has often been suggested that Loki may be referring to rivers flowing into the sea, which is of course Njörðr's special domain, but if so then Loki's mental processes are shown as bizarre to the point of insanity. Njörðr ignores the last claim completely, pointing out only that although sent to the gods as a hostage, he differs from Loki in being manly, and the father of the heroic Freyr.

Loki replies that Freyr was the product of incest. Since we know from *Heimskringla* that marriage with close relatives was a Vanir custom, Loki is merely exhibiting yet again his paucity of imagination. At this stage he is unable even to pretend to find any fault in Freyr's character.

Týr presses this point home by continuing the praise of Freyr that Njörðr had begun. One could and should ask why it is Týr who speaks at this stage. Perhaps the reason is that, according to *Hymiskviða*, Týr is Hymir's son. A more obvious reason for Týr to speak up is that Loki seems to be running out of steam. Who better to revive his malice than the god responsible for binding Fenrir?

Once again, Loki is unable to respond to the points made in Freyr's favour. Predictably, though, he takes the bait and turns bitterly on Týr, who he says has never been a reconciler of "two parties in a dispute", and who, moreover, lost his hand in binding Fenrir. This sounds like whining. Of course Týr's primary role is not to reconcile disputes, and that is not what he is trying to do here. On the other hand, Týr certainly seems to have some connection with justice in a far broader sense than Loki is referring to, and as a patron of war it could be said that he is the ultimate settler of disputes.

Týr's response is in keeping with this role. In effect he reminds Loki that he settled the dispute with Fenrir, even if it did cost him a hand. This reply perhaps also reminds the poem's audience of the absence of Þórr. Týr had willingly broken an oath to Fenrir for the sake of a higher motive, and had been prepared to suffer for this. But as we have seen, the absent Þórr appears to have a special dispensation to break sacred oaths when it comes to destroying the forces of chaos.

Given the triviality and lack of imagination that Loki has exhibited all along, we are not surprised that he now claims to have had a son by Týr's wife, and brags that Týr had never received any compensation for this. McKinnell takes this taunt seriously, suggesting that Týr has been unable to force Loki to pay compensation for a genuine wrong because he is one-handed. It is hard to see why a war god however handicapped should be unable to fight Loki, who is not noted for his personal valour. Also, according to Snorri, being one-handed doesn't prevent Týr fighting Garmr at Ragnarök. Admittedly Snorri provides the only reference to this story, but there is no other reference to Týr's 'wife' anywhere else in the literature, and there is no reason to suppose that he had one in any literal sense. This suggests one of two possibilities. Perhaps the poet put these lines in Loki's mouth to emphasise how far his mind is straying from reality. Alternatively, Loki's allegation might refer to a story or kenning in which something is figuratively referred to as Týr's 'wife'. Either way, the allegation fits what we have learned of Loki's character. He has trouble coming up with anything higher than the cheapest of bar-room insults.

Freyr seems to give support to this interpretation of Loki's last speech by showing impatience with him, taunting him with the memory of his bound son and suggesting that this will be Loki's own fate. Loki replies that Freyr is lustful (what else?), and will pay for the loss of his sword at Ragnarök. While the link between Freyr's lost sword and his defeat by Surtr is confirmed by Snorri, what Loki is apparently unaware of (or else has forgotten in the heat of the moment) is that when Surtr's flame is finally extinguished *(Vafprúdnismál* 50) it will be seen not to have destroyed the abodes of the gods, but to have purified them for occupation by the rejuvenated race of Æsir. Ragnarök thus becomes the ultimate Pyrrhic victory.

It would be easy enough for Freyr to point this out to Loki, taunting him with his side's ultimate loss as he has already done with his son's binding. Equally, he could be forgiven for losing his temper with Loki altogether and dealing with him there and then. Of all the gods present, Freyr is most renowned as a warrior, a defender of the gods, and especially a leader. In *Lokasenna* 35 he is called "the protector of the gods"; in *Skírnismál 3* he is "the ruler of the host of gods"; and in *Húsdrápa 7* Freyr is said to rule armies. If any of the gods present are likely to resort to force before it is legitimised, Freyr is the obvious candidate.

Perhaps the need to restrain Freyr explains the strange entry of Byggvir into the argument. His threats against Loki are 'comical', to use McKinnell's term, and I suspect that they are meant to be. If Freyr is in danger of losing his self-control and dealing with Loki himself before þórr returns, he will destroy everything that the gods have achieved so far. Byggvir defuses the situation with some light relief, at the same time rather shrewdly, like a Shakespearian jester, parodying Freyr's anger in a display of comical bellicosity.

Loki seems to support this interpretation by expressing contempt for Byggvir. Naturally, though, he can't leave it there. As a patron of barley, Loki says, Byggvir is inadequate. He distributes bread unequally among men, and drink is a cowardly thing that causes men to fight but never joins in.

Conclusion

Loki has given Heimdallr a wonderful opening to suggest that the intruder is only annoying the gods because he is drunk. Following Loki's last statement, the implication seems to be that Loki wouldn't even dare to be there unless he was pumped up with Dutch courage. McKinnell asks why it should be Heimdallr who intervenes here, apart from the fact that he is Loki's archetypal enemy. Perhaps that is the precise reason. If Freyr is still likely to endanger the gods' purpose, Heimdallr's intervention at this point can only serve to remind Freyr (and the listeners) that it is Heimdallr himself who will ultimately deal with Loki at Ragnarok.

Loki reproaches Heimdallr with being the watchman of the Æsir, a puzzling accusation in itself, and accuses him of having a muddy back. McKinnell discusses what this could mean, and among other possibilities he "tentatively suggests" that this may be a reference to muddy giants having already gained access to Ásgarðr behind Heimdallr's back. If Loki's taunt is meant to have any meaning that we can relate to the known facts, this seems as sound an idea as any. After all, Loki himself gained access to Ásgarðr despite the fact that he is half giant, while a full-blooded giant, in the form of Skaði, is standing right beside them in Ægir's hall. It would be typical of Loki to trivialise Heimdallr's general role as watchman by raising these two particular exceptions. As McKinnell comments, "Such an implication would of course be unfair ... But Loki's slurs do not have to be fair ..."

Skaði acts consistently with this interpretation by speaking next, bluntly telling Loki exactly what fate he can expect. Either Loki knows this already or he is indifferent to it. He replies that he was prominent in the killing of her father. When Skaði then swears eternal enmity to him, Loki claims that she once invited him into her bed. As with the matter of Týr's wife this incident is mentioned nowhere else. It has the ring of being just another of Loki's crude inventions.

All the major gods and goddesses – bar two – have now had their say. The listeners to the poem have been reminded (by Frigg and Týr) of Þórr's absence, but everyone knows that Þórr seldom stays away for long when action is required. His return is now overdue, and there is perhaps no-one better able to remind us a third time than his wife Sif.

Sif's intervention may seem puzzling, but from an artistic point of view it is masterful. Instead of abusing Loki, she offers him a foaming cup of mead and challenges him to find any fault in her.

Loki replies that the two were once lovers. Unlike his earlier unsubstantiated claim along these lines with regard to Týr's wife, this allegation seems to refer to *Hárbarðsljóð* (where it is rejected by Þórr). However we may be expected to regard Loki's claim, the listener should not have forgotten Loki's earlier taunt that Týr had been unable to obtain compensation, and the tension within the poem is suddenly heightened. Whether the claim about Sif is correct or not, Þórr must now have a real case for compensation, either for something that really happened or else for defamation. He is just the god to extract it from Loki. Where is he?

Beyla, who appears to be a patron of animal husbandry, answers immediately. She hears the mountains tremble, and asserts that Þórr is returning to silence he who "defames" or "slanders" both gods and men.

Loki doesn't seem to understand his position. He says Beyla is a milkmaid who is spattered with dung. Being spattered with dung may be a common event in the life of a dairy farmer, but Loki has not merely descended to his lowest level of banality. One other character has previously been accused of serving as a milkmaid, and if Loki were spattered with dung while sexually servicing giants during this escapade, it was at a level of dishonour many rungs lower than would apply to a mere occupational hazard of an honest role in dairy farming.

Loki has run out of ideas, and his challenge to the Æsir has spluttered out ignominiously with a reminder of his own disgrace. He is ready for binding. At this second climax in the poem, Þórr enters, and not before time tells Loki to be quiet. In the next few exchanges, Þórr threatens to destroy Loki, while Loki tries to deter him by recalling earlier occasions on which Þórr may have been afraid. It is a one-sided contest. There is no mythological reason why Þórr should not be afraid from time to time, as long as he overcomes any such fear and triumphs in his duty; but his repeated threats against Loki are clearly taking their toll. Finally Loki acknowledges what the listeners have known all along: Þórr's threats are genuine. Loki runs away, out from the former sanctuary of Ægir's hall, hurling final curses at Ægir over his shoulder.

Loki's humiliation is complete. Despite his earlier bravado toward Bragi, who was restrained by legal considerations, he is now exposed as a coward who has no intention of facing up to a real fight. Loki runs, but of course he is easily subdued and bound with the guts of his son, as Skaði had foretold. There he will remain until Ragnarök, and after hearing *Lokasenna* none could doubt that he deserves this treatment.

Bibliography

Bellows, H.A., 1923, *The Poetic Edda, translated from the Icelandic with an Introduction and Notes.*

Klingenberg, H., 1983, 'Types of Eddic Mythological Poetry', in *Edda: A Collection of Essays* (eds. R.J. Glendinning & H. Bessason).

McKinnell, J., 1987-8, 'Motivation in Lokasenna', *Saga Book XXII*, nos. 3-4, pp. 234-262.

McKinnell, J., 1994, *Both One And Many. Essays on Change and Varieiy in Late Norse Heathenism.*

Meulengracht Sorenson, Preben, 1983, *The Unmanly Man. Concepts of sexual defamation in early Northern Society.* (1980 translation by J. Turville-Petre).

Meulengracht Sorenson, Preben, 1988, *'Loki's senna in Ægir's Hall',* in *Idee. Gestalt. Geschichte. Festchrift Klaus von See. Studien Zur europäischen Kulturtraditian,* (ed. G.W. Weber).

Sveinsson, E., 1962, *lslenzkar bókmenntir i fornold*

Lokasenna

translated by Henry Adams Bellows

Ægir, who was also called Gymir, had prepared ale for the gods, after he had got the mighty kettle, as now has been told. To this feast came Othin and Frigg, his wife. Thor came not, as he was on a journey in the East. Sif, Thor's wife, was there, and Brag, with Ithun, his wife. Tyr, who had but one hand, was there; the wolf Fenrir had bitten off his other hand when they had bound him. There were Njorth and Skathi his wife, Freyr and Freyja, and Vithar, the son of Othin. Loki was there, and Freyr's servants Byggvir and Beyla. Many were there of the gods and elves.

Ægir had two serving-men, Fimafeng and Eldir. Glittering gold they had in place of firelight; the ale came in of itself; and great was the peace. The guests praised much the ability of Ægir's serving-men. Loki might not endure that, and he slew Fimafeng. Then the gods shook their shields and howled at Loki and drove him away to the forest, and thereafter set to drinking again. Loki turned back, and outside he met Eldir. Loki spoke to him:

1. "Speak now, Eldir, | for not one step
Farther shalt thou fare;
What ale-talk here | do they have within,
The sons of the glorious gods?"

Eldir spake:
2. "Of their weapons they talk, | and their might in war,
The sons of the glorious gods;
From the gods and elves | who are gathered here
No friend in words shalt thou find."

Loki spake:
3. "In shall I go | into Ægir's hall,
For the feast I fain would see;
Bale and hatred | I bring to the gods,
And their mead with venom I mix."

Eldir spake:
4. "If in thou goest | to Ægir's hall,
And fain the feast wouldst see,
And with slander and spite | wouldst sprinkle the gods,
Think well lest they wipe it on thee."

Loki spake:
5. "Bethink thee, Eldir, | if thou and I
Shall strive with spiteful speech;
Richer I grow | in ready words
If thou speakest too much to me."

Then Loki went into the hall, but when they who were there saw
who had entered, they were all silent.

Loki spake:
6. "Thirsty I come | into this thine hall,
I, Lopt, from a journey long,
To ask of the gods | that one should give
Fair mead for a drink to me.

7. "Why sit ye silent, | swollen with pride,
Ye gods, and no answer give?
At your feast a place | and a seat prepare me,
Or bid me forth to fare."

Bragi spake:
8. "A place and a seat | will the gods prepare
No more in their midst for thee;
For the gods know well | what men they wish
To find at their mighty feasts."

Loki spake:
9. "Remember, Othin, | in olden days
That we both our blood have mixed;
Then didst thou promise | no ale to pour,
Unless it were brought for us both."

Othin spake:
10. "Stand forth then, Vithar, | and let the wolf's father
Find a seat at our feast;
Lest evil should Loki | speak aloud
Here within Ægir's hall."

Then Vithar arose and poured drink for Loki; but before he drank he
spoke to the gods:
11. "Hail to you, gods! | ye goddesses, hail!
Hail to the holy throng!

Save for the god | who yonder sits,
Bragi there on the bench."

Bragi spake:
12. "A horse and a sword | from my hoard will I give,
And a ring gives Bragi to boot,
That hatred thou mak'st not | among the gods;
So rouse not the great ones to wrath."

Loki spake:
13. "In horses and rings | thou shalt never be rich,
Bragi, but both shalt thou lack;
Of the gods and elves | here together met
Least brave in battle art thou,
(And shyest thou art of the shot.)"

Bragi spake:
14. "Now were I without | as I am within,
And here in Ægir's hall,
Thine head would I bear | in mine hands away,
And pay thee the price of thy lies."

Loki spake:
15. "In thy seat art thou bold, | not so are thy deeds,
Bragi, adorner of benches!
Go out and fight | if angered thou feelest,
No hero such forethought has."

Ithun spake:
16. "Well, prithee, Bragi, | his kinship weigh,
Since chosen as wish-son he was;
And speak not to Loki | such words of spite
Here within Ægir's hall."

Loki spake:
17. "Be silent, Ithun! | thou art, I say,
Of women most lustful in love,
Since thou thy washed-bright | arms didst wind
About thy brother's slayer."

Ithun spake:
18. "To Loki I speak not | with spiteful words
Here within Ægir's hall;
And Bragi I calm, | who is hot with beer,
For I wish not that fierce they should fight."

Gefjun spake:
19. "Why, ye gods twain, | with bitter tongues
Raise hate among us here?

28

Loki is famed | for his mockery foul,
And the dwellers in heaven he hates."

Loki spake:
20. "Be silent, Gefjun! | for now shall I say
Who led thee to evil life;
The boy so fair | gave a necklace bright,
And about him thy leg was laid."
Othin spake:
21. "Mad art thou, Loki, | and little of wit,
The wrath of Gefjun to rouse;
For the fate that is set | for all she sees,
Even as I, methinks."

Loki spake:
22. "Be silent, Othin! | not justly thou settest
The fate of the fight among men;
Oft gav'st thou to him | who deserved not the gift,
To the baser, the battle's prize."

Othin spake:
23. "Though I gave to him | who deserved not the gift,
To the baser, the battle's prize;
Winters eight | wast thou under the earth,
Milking the cows as a maid,
(Ay, and babes didst thou bear;
Unmanly thy soul must seem.)"

Loki spake:
24. "They say that with spells | in Samsey once
Like witches with charms did'st thou work;
And in witch's guise | among men didst thou go;
Unmanly thy soul must seem."

Frigg spake:
25. "Of the deeds ye two | of old have done
Ye should make no speech among men;
Whate'er ye have done | in days gone by,
Old tales should ne'er be told."

Loki spake:
26. "Be silent, Frigg! | thou art Fjorgyn's wife,
But ever lustful in love;
For Vili and Ve, | thou wife of Vithrir,
Both in thy bosom have lain."

Frigg spake:
27. "If a son like Baldr | were by me now,
Here within Ægir's hall,

From the sons of the gods | thou should'st go not forth
Till thy fierceness in fight were tried."

Loki spake:
28. "Thou wilt then, Frigg, | that further I tell
Of the ill that now I know;
Mine is the blame | that Baldr no more
Thou see'st ride home to the hall."
Freyja spake:
29. "Mad art thou, Loki, | that known thou makest
The wrong and shame thou hast wrought;
The fate of all | does Frigg know well,
Though herself she says it not."

Loki spake:
30. "Be silent, Freyja! | for fully I know thee,
Sinless thou art not thyself;
Of the gods and elves | who are gathered here,
Each one as thy lover has lain."

Freyja spake:
31. "False is thy tongue, | and soon shalt thou find
That it sings thee an evil song;
The gods are wroth, | and the goddesses all,
And in grief shalt thou homeward go."

Loki spake:
32. "Be silent, Freyja! | thou foulest witch,
And steeped full sore in sin;
In the arms of thy brother | the bright gods caught thee
When Freyja her wind set free."

Njorth spake:
33. "Small ill does it work | though a woman may have
A lord or a lover or both;
But a wonder it is | that this womanish god
Comes hither, though babes he has borne."

Loki spake:
34. "Be silent, Njorth; | thou wast eastward sent,
To the gods as a hostage given;
And the daughters of Hymir | their privy had
When use did they make of thy mouth."

Njorth spake:
35. "Great was my gain, | though long was I gone,
To the gods as a hostage given;
The son did I have | whom no man hates,
And foremost of gods is found."

Loki spake:
36. "Give heed now, Njorth, | nor boast too high,
No longer I hold it hid;
With thy sister had'st thou | so fair a son,
Thus had'st thou no worse a hope."
Tyr spake:
37. "Of the heroes brave | is Freyr the best
Here in the home of the gods;
He harms not maids | nor the wives of men,
And the bound from their fetters he frees."

Loki spake:
38. "Be silent, Tyr! | for between two men
Friendship thou ne'er could'st fashion;
Fain would I tell | how Fenrir once
Thy right hand rent from thee."

Tyr spake:
39. "My hand do I lack, | but Hrothvitnir thou,
And the loss brings longing to both;
Ill fares the wolf | who shall ever await
In fetters the fall of the gods."

Loki spake:
40. "Be silent, Tyr! | for a son with me
Thy wife once chanced to win;
Not a penny, methinks, | wast thou paid for the wrong,
Nor wast righted an inch, poor wretch."

Freyr spake:
41. "By the mouth of the river | the wolf remains
Till the gods to destruction go;
Thou too shalt soon, | if thy tongue is not stilled,
Be fettered, thou forger of ill."

Loki spake:
42. "The daughter of Gymir | with gold didst thou buy,
And sold thy sword to boot;
But when Muspell's sons | through Myrkwood ride,
Thou shalt weaponless wait, poor wretch."

Byggvir spake:
43. "Had I birth so famous | as Ingunar-Freyr,
And sat in so lofty a seat,
I would crush to marrow | this croaker of ill,
And beat all his body to bits."

31

Loki spake:
44. "What little creature | goes crawling there,
Snuffling and snapping about?
At Freyr's ears ever | wilt thou be found,
Or muttering hard at the mill."

Byggvir spake:
45. "Byggvir my name, | and nimble am I,
As gods and men do grant;
And here am I proud | that the children of Hropt
Together all drink ale."

Loki spake:
46. "Be silent, Byggvir! | thou never could'st set
Their shares of the meat for men;
Hid in straw on the floor, | they found thee not
When heroes were fain to fight."

Heimdall spake:
47. "Drunk art thou, Loki, | and mad are thy deeds,
Why, Loki, leav'st thou this not?
For drink beyond measure | will lead all men
No thought of their tongues to take."

Loki spake:
48. "Be silent, Heimdall! | in days long since
Was an evil fate for thee fixed;
With back held stiff | must thou ever stand,
As warder of heaven to watch."

Skathi spake:
49. "Light art thou, Loki, | but longer thou may'st not
In freedom flourish thy tail;
On the rocks the gods bind thee | with bowels torn
Forth from thy frost-cold son."

Loki spake:
50. "Though on rocks the gods bind me | with bowels torn
Forth from my frost-cold son,
I was first and last | at the deadly fight
There where Thjazi we caught."

Skathi spake:
51. "Wert thou first and last | at the deadly fight
There where Thjazi was caught,
From my dwellings and fields | shall ever come forth
A counsel cold for thee."

Loki spake:
52. "More lightly thou spakest | with Laufey's son,

When thou bad'st me come to thy bed;
Such things must be known | if now we two
Shall seek our sins to tell."

Then Sif came forward and poured mead for Loki in a crystal cup,
and said:
53. "Hail too thee, Loki, | and take thou here
The crystal cup of old mead;
For me at least, | alone of the gods,
Blameless thou knowest to be."

He took the horn, and drank therefrom:
54. "Alone thou wert | if truly thou would'st
All men so shyly shun;
But one do I know | full well, methinks,
Who had thee from Hlorrithi's arms,-
(Loki the crafty in lies.)"

Beyla spake:
55. "The mountains shake, | and surely I think
From his home comes Hlorrithi now;
He will silence the man | who is slandering here
Together both gods and men."

Loki spake:
56. "Be silent, Beyla! | thou art Byggvir's wife,
And deep art thou steeped in sin;
A greater shame | to the gods came ne'er,
Befouled thou art with thy filth."

Then came Thor forth, and spake:
57. "Unmanly one, cease, | or the mighty hammer,
Mjollnir, shall close thy mouth;
Thy shoulder-cliff | shall I cleave from thy neck,
And so shall thy life be lost."

Loki spake:
58. "Lo, in has come | the son of Earth:
Why threaten so loudly, Thor?
Less fierce thou shalt go | to fight with the wolf
When he swallows Sigfather up."

Thor spake:
59. "Unmanly one, cease, | or the mighty hammer,
Mjollnir, shall close thy mouth;
I shall hurl thee up | and out in the East,
Where men shall see thee no more."

Loki spake:

60. "That thou hast fared | on the East-road forth
To men should'st thou say no more;
In the thumb of a glove | did'st thou hide, thou great one,
And there forgot thou wast Thor."

Thor spake:

61. "Unmanly one, cease, | or the mighty hammer,
Mjollnir, shall close thy mouth;
My right hand shall smite thee | with Hrungnir's slayer,
Till all thy bones are broken."

Loki spake:

62. "A long time still | do I think to live,
Though thou threatenest thus with thy hammer;
Rough seemed the straps | of Skrymir's wallet,
When thy meat thou mightest not get,
(And faint from hunger didst feel.)"

Thor spake:

63. "Unmanly one, cease, | or the mighty hammer,
Mjollnir, shall close thy mouth;
The slayer of Hrungnir | shall send thee to hell,
And down to the gate of death."

Loki spake:

64. "I have said to the gods | and the sons of the god,
The things that whetted my thoughts;
But before thee alone | do I now go forth,
For thou fightest well, I ween.
65. "Ale hast thou brewed, | but, Ægir, now
Such feasts shalt thou make no more;
O'er all that thou hast | which is here within
Shall play the flickering flames,
(And thy back shall be burnt with fire.)"

And after that Loki hid himself in Franang's waterfall in the guise of a salmon, and there the gods took him. He was bound with the bowels of his son Vali, but his son Narfi was changed to a wolf. Skathi took a poison-snake and fastened it up over Loki's face, and the poison dropped thereon. Sigyn, Loki's wife, sat there and held a shell under the poison, but when the shell was full she bore away the poison, and meanwhile the poison dropped on Loki. Then he struggled so hard that the whole earth shook therewith; and now that is called an earthquake.